99 Snippets of... *Kickboxing*

99 Snippets of... *Kickboxing*

Alexandra Barnett

DRAGON SNAKE PUBLISHING

Published by Dragon Snake Publishing

Dragon Snake Publishing is an imprint of
The Dragon Snake Company Ltd
Stonehill Farm
Charlton
Malmesbury
Wiltshire SN16 9DY

www.dragonsnakepublishing.co.uk

Cover photography by Sarah Knights
www.sarahknightsphotography.com

British Library Cataloguing in Publication Data.
A catalogue record for this book is available from the British Library.

ISBN: 978-0-9571706-0-5

Printed and bound in Great Britain by Printondemand-Worldwide

DEDICATION

To my Mum and Dad who have been my inspiration and motivation. To Anna who has supported me over the years and to Laurence, my instructor who has been my martial arts mentor.

CONTENTS

PART 1: EQUiPMENT

PART 2: MOVES

PART 3: BITS & PIECES

PART 1:

EQUIPMENT

1

BAG GLOVES

Bag gloves are similar to boxing gloves except that they have a lot less padding, especially around the thumb and palm of the hand. Bag gloves can cover the fingers, but there are also fingerless bag gloves available where the fingers are exposed. Bag gloves are useful when a practitioner does not want a lot of padding as they give flexibility to manoeuvre much more easily, useful for some moves or attacks. Bag gloves are not used in Kickboxing competitions as they do not have enough protection.

2

BOB®

BOB® (Body Opponent Bag) is a workout bag made by Century. The bag is moulded like a man's torso to be more lifelike than standard punch bags. The advantage of practicing moves on BOB® is that accuracy can be improved and it gives people an idea of what it is like to hit a person shaped figure rather than a normal punch bag or pads.

3

BOXING GLOVES

Boxing gloves are padded or cushioned gloves that are used to protect the hands during a fight or normal training. There are a variety of boxing gloves available with different weights depending on their intended use. Common weights for boxing gloves are 10, 12, 14 and 16 oz, but heavier and lighter gloves are also available. 6 oz gloves are usually designed for children and are much smaller in size. Cheaper gloves are made of PU "leather" and more expensive gloves are made of a type of leather e.g. cows hide leather.

4

CHEST PROTECTOR

Chest protectors are a form of body protection largely aimed at female martial artists. They come in different versions but one popular variety consists of a LYCRA® crop top with a large 'pocket' and a strong, flexible polyethylene protector that inserts into the crop top. They are very effective and quite comfortable to wear. A second type consists of the guard which has adjustable elastic straps attached to it. There are also male versions though these are more commonly worn in fencing.

LYCRA® is a trademark of INVISTA.

5

CONTACT TROUSERS

Contact trousers are the traditional trousers worn by kick boxers. They are also one half of a Gi which is worn in other martial arts including: Judo, MMA, Jiu-Jitsu, Karate and Taekwondo. They allow for flexibility which is important for high kicks. Contact trousers are commonly made of polycotton, cotton or satin. They sometimes have stripes and/or piping down the sides and the club's logo or name on them.

6

FOCUS PADS

Focus pads are usually made of leather (or fake leather), either curved or straight and are slightly larger than a hand. They are used for people to practice punching. One person must hold the focus pads while their partner punches. Unlike a punch bag, they are used to focus on the speed rather than the power of the attacks. Focus pads are also known as Hook & Jab Pads.

7

FOOT GUARDS

Foot guards are used to protect the feet when sparring. They are padded or cushioned protective equipment that are shaped like boots. They have elasticated straps with hook and loop fasteners that strap around the middle of the foot to keep them securely fastened.

8

GROIN GUARD

Groin guards are a must when sparring or competing in Kickboxing. They are available from martial arts stockists in both male and female versions. Groin guards resemble underwear but with extra padding where needed.

9

GUM SHIELD

A gum shield is not a piece of equipment that is made specifically for Kickboxing, but it is a must for anyone who wants to spar or compete. Gum shields protect the teeth from any impact they might incur during activity. Sparring has a high probability of causing an impact to the teeth. There are two options for gum shields. One option is to get your dentist to make one which is exactly fitted to match your teeth, the other option is to buy an off the shelf version. The dentist made gum shields are more expensive but will provide better protection, the off the shelf ones are fairly cheap and easy to obtain.

10

HAND WRAPS

Hand wraps are made of cotton, usually with a hook and loop fasteners. The idea is for martial artists to have material they can wrap around both their hands and wrists in order to either give them extra protection when wearing boxing gloves or to give them protection when not wearing boxing gloves. Not only do they protect hands, but they reinforce the wrist by keeping it straight. When a practitioner punches, they must keep their wrist straight to minimise sustaining an injury. Hand wraps are a perfect way to help reduce the likelihood of an injury to the wrist.

11

HANGING BAG

Hanging bags are either hung with chains from the ceiling, from punch bag stands or wall brackets. Standard hanging bags are cylindrical in shape. Other variants of hanging bags include uppercut bags (funnel shaped), hook and jab bags (pear shaped) and ball shaped bags.

12

HEAD GUARD

Head guards are cushioned and padded products that give a degree of protection to the head. The level of protection is dependent on the type of head guard used. There are partial head guards and full head guards. Partial head guards tend to cover the top of the head and partially cover the sides. A full head guard covers everything that the partial guard covers plus completely covering the sides of the face.

13

HOOK & JAB PADS

Hook & jab pads is another term used for focus pads. They are usually made of leather (or fake leather) and are the pads used for people to practice their punching. One person must hold the hook & jab pads while their partner punches. Unlike a punch bag, they are used to focus on the speed rather than the power of the attacks.

14

KICK SHIELD

Kick shields are large rectangular, cushioned pads. They are designed for practicing kicks, but can also be used for punches. They are similar to Thai pads except that the pad holder only requires one kick shield instead of two Thai pads. Kick shields are great for standard kicks e.g. front kicks, side kicks, roundhouse kicks and back kicks. However, Thai pads are best used for more advanced kicks such as hook kicks, snap roundhouse kicks, spinning hook kicks and spinning axe kicks. This is because a kick shield is too big for the pad holder to effectively hold the pad in the correct position for the more advanced kicks.

15

PUNCH BAG

Punch bags are used to practice punches and kicks, improve power and help physical performance. There are many different types of bags and several methods of construction. Some are filled with sand and are covered in leather or a synthetic equivalent. These bags usually hang from the ceiling or wall. Variations of hanging bags are ones that can be used to practice uppercuts. These bags have a larger diameter at the top and smaller at the bottom. Traditional bags have the same diameter throughout. Freestanding bags are a flexible alternative. They usually have a plastic base which can be filled with water or sand.

16

RiNG

A ring is an area used for fights or sparring and competitions. A ring is usually square with four posts at each corner and rope around each post to create a barrier around the ring. There are seats in a couple of corners that are diagonally opposite each other. The seats are for the competitors between rounds.

17

SHADOWBOXER®

The ShadowBoxer® is a martial arts and fitness aid which comprises of a resistance belt and rubber resistance bands. Resistance bands are available for both arm and legs enabling a full body workout if required. It is a useful training aid when travelling or training alone.

18

SHiN PADS

Shin pads are used for martial arts solely to protect your shins. They are usually elasticated padding that can just be slipped on - no straps. Some shin pads are made of foam instead of elasticated padding and require hook and loop fastening straps for attaching to the leg.

19

SHIN/INSTEP PADS

Shin/instep pads protect both the shin and the foot. They are very similar to the shin pads: elasticated for slipping over the foot and leg. Some shin/instep pads are made of foam instead of elasticated padding and require hook and loop fastening straps for attaching to the leg.

20

SPEED BALL

Speed balls are much smaller than punch bags and are inflated rather than filled with materials. Speed balls move very fast and are good for martial artists who are trying to improve their reaction skills, speed and eye coordination. There are different varieties of speed balls. Some hang from platforms which are circular and hang on the wall. Others are suspended with rope or straps that hang from the ceiling and rise up from the floor (tension in the bottom strap is created from a weighted disc on the floor).

21

STANDALONE BAG

Standalone bags come in different shapes and sizes, but have a plastic, cylindrical base. The base is hollow and requires the user to fill it up with either water or sand in order to keep it in place. Standalone bags are excellent for people who are unable to hang a bag from the wall or ceiling.

22

THAI PADS

Thai pads usually come in pairs as they are not as large as kick shields. They are rectangular in shape and are either flat or curved. They are made of leather or PU "leather" and have straps on the back for the holder to strap their arms into. They are designed to take the impact of punches and kicks.

PART 2:

MOVES

23

AXE KICK

Axe kicks are one of the few kicks where gravity does a lot of the work for you. The motion of an axe kick is very much like the motion of a real axe used to chop wood or something similar. Using a real axe, the user would lift the axe up high and then let it drop vertically downwards to chop the wood. With the axe kick, the practitioner lifts their leg as high as they can, or as high as is necessary, and then lets it drop, using the heel of their foot to make contact with their opponent.

24

BACK KICK

The Back kick is also known as a spinning back kick. The kick is performed with the attacker's back to their opponent. A back kick can either be started by shifting the lead leg across your body or by raising the heel of the lead foot so that you are on the tip of your toes. Then the attacker spins 180 degrees so that their back is facing their opponent and kicks with either a vertical foot or a horizontal foot. Once the attack has been made, the attacker can either continue spinning in the direction they are going and face the way they started or they can come back on themselves by spinning 180 degrees in the opposite direction to face the way they started.

25

BLOCK

Blocks are defences against punches, kicks and other attacks which come in a variety of forms. A block could be a crush against a roundhouse kick or a parry against a cross. A block is the term used for referring to a method of preventing an attack from succeeding.

26

BOB & WEAVE DRILLS

Bob & weave drills are combinations (usually punches) that also include weaving. If this was being demonstrated with a pad holder, the pad holder would throw out one of the pads towards the attacker (usually a wide cross or hook) which forces the attacker to defend with a weave. The movement of a weave is in a 'u' shape. If a wide cross is coming towards the defender, they bend down, move their upper body to the left and rise upwards. When weaving, it is important to not look at the floor as the defender cannot see exactly what their opponent is doing and could get hit. An example of a bob & weave drill would be: jab, cross, weave, cross, hook, cross.

27

CATCH

A catch is a defence move used in Kickboxing quite a lot. When an opponent jabs, the martial artist defending can turn their boxing glove to catch the punch. The advantage of this defence move is that it can be done very quickly which is particularly useful if the opponent has punched very fast. However, a catch cannot be used against a cross because crosses are one of the most powerful punches and a catch can sometimes be too feeble to protect against such a strong punch.

28

COMBINATIONS

Combinations consist of combining different moves into one drill. For example: jab, cross, roundhouse kick; jab, front kick, back kick, roundhouse kick. Combinations can be more traditional set moves or could be made up using any of the moves a Kickboxing practitioner knows.

29

COVER

The term cover can be applied to defend against different punches and kicks. One example of a cover is against uppercuts where the defender puts both forearms and fists together to stop the uppercut from hitting their face. A second example is where the defender drops their height slightly to use their guard to cover their body from a body hook.

30

CROSS

The cross is a straight, right-handed punch (if the practitioner is right-handed). It is usually stronger than the jab (but not necessarily) and quick. To improve the power of the cross, the practitioner will pivot on their rear foot (and turn the upper body) so that the knee and toes are pointing in the direction of the punch as the fist makes contact with the target.

31

CRUSH

The crush is a defence technique which is commonly used to defend against roundhouse kicks, but is also used for other attacks. An outside crush, for example, involves the defender raising their knee up to make a 90 degree angle with their waist and pointing their knee to the side rather than in front of them. This results in the shins connecting when the attacker attacks with a roundhouse kick. Shin pads or shin/instep pads are required for this move as shin to shin contact can cause pain and injury if the attack is strong.

32

DOUBLE JAB

See 'jab' for information on a single jab. A double jab is two consecutive jabs. After the first jab, the attacker can either pull their hand all the way back to their guard position before the second jab or pull their hand back about halfway. The choice is down to the preference of the practitioner.

33

DUCK

A duck can be applied to any attacks for example, jabs and crosses. The defender bends their legs and lowers their body to the point where their head is below the attack. It is important not to look down at the floor when ducking, though, because the defender may miss other attacks and won't be ready to defend them.

34

ELBOW CRUSH

An elbow crush is a form of defence against jabs and crosses. Imagine there is a line drawn down through the centre of the face. The practitioner would raise their hand up that line and continue over the top of the head until they can grab the back of their head. The elbow should end up in front of the face. This results in the arm and elbow protecting the face from attack. If done accurately, the attacker's fist should hit the defender's elbow.

35

FOOTWORK

Footwork is a broad term that can cover a variety of different 'step' techniques. Martial arts can differ in the forms of footwork used depending on what is effective for a particular move. Kickboxing tends to lend itself to quite simple Footwork: stepping forwards, backwards, sideways and pivoting. Footwork is very important in Kickboxing and especially at speed as this can help to give an advantage to a kick boxer over their opponent when sparring.

36

FRONT KICK

Front kicks can be done off both the lead leg and the rear leg.

Rear leg: When doing a front kick off the rear leg, the attacker will bring their rear leg up so that their knee is at a right angle to their waist and kick to the body or head using the ball of their foot. It is important not to kick with the toes as this could result in breaking them.

Lead leg: Lead leg front kicks are almost the same as rear leg barring the footwork before the attack is made. When doing a lead leg front kick, the attacker must first step their rear foot up to their lead foot, then bring the knee of the lead leg up, in line with the waist, and kick with the ball of the foot.

37

GUARD

The guard in Kickboxing plays a key part in the defence of the practitioner. In Kickboxing, the guard height can vary from having the hands around chin height all the way up to forehead height. In Kickboxing the fists are positioned so that the curled fingers are facing each other. When an attacker kicks, they sometimes start with their guard higher in anticipation of the guard being lowered once the kick is made. There is a natural tendency to lower the guard for kicks. The guard is always kept up when an attack is not being made at that time. After each punch, for example, the attacker must bring their fist back to the guard position straight away. Note: when an attacker punches with one hand, they still need to keep the other hand up in the guard position.

38

HOOK

Hooks come in a variety of different shapes and sizes. There are hooks from both the lead and rear hands as well as hooks to the body and head.

Head Hooks: Head hooks make contact with the side of the opponent's head. The attacker's arm arcs round almost like the shape of a hook. To make the hook more effective and to prevent shoulder and knee problems, the attacker must pivot their foot 90 degrees in the direction of the punch. For example, a right-hander attacking with a lead hook will pivot their lead foot (left) 90 degrees to the right.

Body Hooks: Body hooks are much the same as head hooks except they involve the attacker bending down so that their elbow can touch the top of their leg before they do the hook to the side of the body. Shovel hooks are another form of body hook that do not require the attacker to bend as low to make the punch. The direction of attack for a shovel hook is more diagonally upwards than a body hook. The aim of a shovel hook is to make contact with the bottom of the ribs.

39

HOOK KICK

The shape of the leg during a hook kick is similar to the shape of the arm during a hook punch. Hook kicks can be done from both the lead and the rear legs. The attacker makes contact with the side of the opponent's head or body using the heel of the foot. The attacker lifts their knee up and pivots as much as is necessary on the other foot, then hooks the back of their foot round to make contact.

40

INSIDE TRIPLE

An inside triple is a form of defence or counter attack drill that can be done as part of training. The attacker either attacks with a jab or cross. The opponent defends with an outside parry and jab or cross to the body. The defender then follows up with three punches to the attacker.

41

LEAD HAND/FOOT

For right-handed people, the lead hand and foot are the left hand and foot. For left-handed people, they are the right hand and foot. The leads are designed more for speed rather than power. The reason for this is the leads are usually the practitioner's weakest and therefore will never have the power of the rears. Also, as a result of the Kickboxing stance, the leads are closer to the opponent automatically making them the quickest.

42

JAB

The jab is a straight, left-handed punch (if the practitioner is right-handed). It is usually weaker than the cross, but can be developed to be a lot quicker which is effective in some fighting scenarios. The jab does not tend to have as much body movement as other punches, however, it is important to turn the body into the punch to try and get as much power out of the punch as possible.

43

JUMPING BACK KICK

A Jumping back kick is very similar to a normal back kick or spinning back kick (see back kick). The only difference is the addition of a jump. In Kickboxing, jumps are not required to be very high because, too much energy would go into the jump and not the kick. Different styles of Kickboxing approach jumping kicks in a different way. The focus here will be on vertical jumps. The jump occurs at the point the kick is made. Once the attacker has turned 180 degrees, the kick is carried out with the rear leg and the jump is executed on the lead leg.

44

JUMPING FRONT KICK

(See front kick for information on standard front kick). The style of Kickboxing here uses vertical jumps. Jumping front kicks are normally executed on the rear leg. The jump is made using the lead leg as the rear has come up to kick. The added jump to the kick gives a little bit more power and distance to the kick.

45

JUMPING ROUNDHOUSE KICK

(See roundhouse kick for information on standard roundhouse kick). Jumping roundhouse kicks where the jump is vertical will be focused on here. The vertical jump occurs at the point where the kicking leg is already in motion to make contact with the opponent. As with roundhouse kicks, the jumping leg still needs to pivot about 90 degrees.

46

JUMPING SIDE KICK

(See side kick for information on standard side kick). The vertical jump version of the jumping side kick is described. The jump in the side kick occurs at the point where the kicking leg is extending. The jump does not need to be very high in order to gain extra power which is channelled through the kick.

47

JUMPING SPINNING AXE KICK

(See spinning axe kick for information on standard spinning axe kick). Kickboxing styles vary but here the jump is vertical. The vertical jump occurs at the point where the attacker has already pivoted most of the 360 degrees, just before the side of the foot strikes.

48

JUMPING SPINNING HOOK KICK

(See spinning hook kick for information on standard spinning hook kick). The vertical jump version is used for this jumping spinning hook kick. The vertical jump occurs at the point where the attacker has already pivoted most of the 360 degrees, just before the heel of the foot strikes.

49

KiCKiNG

Kicking is executed with the legs. Kicks in Kickboxing originate from Muay Thai and Karate. Below are some of the kicks that are used:

- Front Kicks
- Side Kicks
- Back Kicks
- Roundhouse Kicks
- Snap Roundhouse Kicks
- Hook Kicks
- Axe Kicks
- Spinning Axe Kicks
- Spinning Hook Kicks

50

MEDIUM RANGE UPPERCUTS

Medium range uppercuts are executed further away from the opponent compared to close range uppercuts. Uppercuts are aimed at the chin of the opponent. Unlike close range, medium range uppercuts do not require the attacker to bend down as much. The attacker bends their upper body slightly in a north easterly or north westerly direction depending on the fist punching. From this position, the attacker shoots their fist from the guard position straight to the target while twisting their upper body to increase the momentum of the punch. For example, if the left fist is punching then the upper body would turn clockwise.

51

OUTSIDE TRIPLE

An outside triple is a form of defence or counter attack drill that can be done as part of training. The attacker either attacks with a lead head hook or rear head hook. The opponent defends with either a weave or a forearm block and simultaneous punch to the head. The defender then follows up with three punches to the attacker.

52

OVERHAND RIGHT

The overhand right punch uses the cross hand to make the attack. This punch requires the rotation of the shoulder, causing the arm to arc over the shoulder and let gravity pull the hand down to make contact. At the point of contact, the fist should be pointing downwards. If this punch is done against a pad, the pad holder should hold the pad facing upwards (the opposite to holding for an uppercut).

53

PAD HOLDING

Pad holding is where one practitioner holds either hook & jab pads or focus pads, kick shields or Thai pads. Pads are an alternative to punch bags for training purposes. When holding pads, the practitioner has to be careful not to hurt themselves if their partner is quite a strong hitter or kicker. The best way to avoid any injury, especially for punches, is to push the pad towards their partner's fist. This increases the resistance against the impact of the punch. For kicks, it is best to have one leg further back with both legs bent in order to give more stability.

54

PARRY

A parry is one of the defences used against punches e.g. jabs and crosses (straight punches). Example: against a jab (left hand): as the jab comes towards the defender, they use their right hand to push the fist across (towards the left). The exact same process is used against the cross except using opposite hands. Tip: It is important to not push the fist too far across because it opens the defender up for a second attack while their arm is across their body. A small push would be just enough to divert the punch, but maintain a good guard in case a second attack comes.

55

PARTNER WORK

Partner work is the term used for practicing attacking and defence techniques with a partner in a very controlled manner. Partner work usually involves set exercises for the two practitioners to practice together. This gives students a better sense of what might happen in a fight without fighting. They can also hone in their defensive and reactionary skills.

56

PiVOT

A pivot is the rotation of a foot on a single spot. Pivots are commonly used as part of the footwork in Kickboxing. For example, when doing a roundhouse kick, the practitioner should pivot at least 90 degrees on their lead foot; lead hook punches require the lead foot to pivot 90 degrees in the direction of the punch.

57

PUNCHiNG

Punching is executed with the hands. Punches in Kickboxing originate from Boxing. Below are some of the punches that are used:

- Jab
- Cross
- Hook
- Uppercut

58

REAR HAND/FOOT

For right-handed people, the rear hand and foot are the right hand and foot. For left-handed people, they are the left hand and foot. The rears are designed more for power than speed. The reason for this is the rears are usually the practitioner's strongest and therefore will always have more power than the leads. They are not used so much for speed because, as a result of the Kickboxing stance, the rears are further away from the opponent meaning it would take longer for them to reach the opponent than the leads.

59

RIGHT CROSS

Right cross can mean many things, but in this case, it means a cross that has been executed from an angled position. To execute a right cross, the attacker needs to shift to the right (left if left-handed) before crossing their opponent.

60

ROUNDHOUSE KICK

The roundhouse kick is an attack using the shin. The attacker pivots on their lead foot about 90 degrees in order to get momentum behind the kick. The rear leg is quite straight, but there is a slight bend in the leg. Roundhouse kicks are either aimed at the body (rib area) or the head.

61

SCOOPS

Scoops are defensive moves that are usually applied to front kicks and side kicks. When looking at front kicks, scoops can be applied to the inside of the foot or the outside. Outside scoops spin the opponent round and inside scoops open up the legs. For example, if the opponent attacked with a lead leg front kick, the defender would use their lead hand to scoop up the foot, going round the outside of the opponent's foot (outside scoop). The defender would grab hold of the heel and push, causing the opponent to spin.

62

SHADOWBOXING

Shadowboxing is Kickboxing done in the air with no object to hit. Sometimes people do shadowboxing with extra resistance e.g. wrist and ankle weights. Shadowboxing is good for working on technique and speed. It is important when shadowboxing not to overextend the arms and legs otherwise you can damage your joints.

63

SHORT RiGHT

A short right is a cross where the attacker has stepped towards the opponent so that they are close enough together so the cross arm cannot be fully extended (see cross for more information on the cross). If the attacker wants to get more power from the close range cross, they can rotate their shoulder forward and release the punch just as the shoulder rotation ends. The shoulder rotation increases the momentum behind the punch therefore making it more powerful.

64

SIDE KICK

A side kick is an attack where the foot strikes with the sole, but at a horizontal angle. Side kicks are done off both the lead and rear legs. If the practitioner were to execute a rear leg side kick, they would pivot 90 degrees on their lead foot and raise their rear knee (level with their hip) simultaneously. From this position, they lean back and extend their rear leg in order to strike the opponent or pad. The lead leg side kick is the same except the practitioner steps their rear leg up to their lead leg first.

65

SNAP ROUNDHOUSE KICK

Snap roundhouse kicks are commonly aimed at the head of the opponent in Kickboxing. They can be done off both the lead and rear legs. For a rear leg snap roundhouse kick, the attacker pivots their lead foot also raising their rear knee at a slight angle. From there, the attacker can either have pointed toes or flexed toes and kick the head or pad and retracting back to the raised knee position before bringing the foot back to the ground. The kick snaps back after the attack giving it the name snap roundhouse kick. The process is the same for the lead leg except the attacker steps their rear leg up to meet their lead leg first.

66

SLiP

Slips are an evasive move in Kickboxing. Slips are performed to either the right or left of a punch in order to avoid getting hit. It is more common to slip to the outside of a punch in order to get the head out of harm's way. Slipping to the inside could result in getting hit by the opponent's other fist. The slip is executed by leaning to the right or left.

67

SPARRING

Sparring occurs when there is contact between two kick boxers. They usually wear protective gear. Sparring differs from partner work as there are no set combinations in sparring. In Kickboxing, practitioners cannot attack below the waist. People either spar to apply their knowledge to more realistic situations or for preparation for a competition.

68

SPINNING AXE KICK

A spinning axe kick is used to hit the side of an opponent's head. When the attack is executed, the attacker's foot will be flexed upwards and it is the side of the foot that connects with the opponent's head. As this is a spinning kick, the attacker must first make a 360 degree rotation: the attacker shifts their lead foot to the side (towards the direction of the spin) and starts spinning. Once the attacker is past 180 degrees, they start lifting their rear leg up in preparation for the attack. The attacker continues to spin until they make contact with the opponent's head. The spinning axe kick is very similar to the spinning hook kick except the part of the foot that makes contact with the head. This kick can be done off both legs, however, some clubs focus only on the strongest leg or side.

69

SPINNING BACK KICK

The spinning back kick is also known as a back kick. The kick is performed with the attacker's back to their opponent. A back kick can either be started by shifting the lead leg across your body or by raising the heel of the lead foot so that you are on the tip of your toes. Then the attacker spins 180 degrees so that their back is facing their opponent and kicks with either a vertical foot or a horizontal foot. Once the attack has been made, the attacker can either continue spinning in the direction they are going and face the way they started or they can come back on themselves by spinning 180 degrees in the opposite direction to face the way they started.

70

SPiNNiNG BACK FiST

A spinning back fist is usually done off the rear hand. The attacker shifts their lead leg to the side (in the direction of the spin). They spin around 360 degrees, but before they finish the spin, they extend their rear arm out towards the opponent. Without completely straightening the arm, attacker connects their back knuckles to the side of the opponent's head. It is important not to completely straighten the arm when attacking because it can cause damage to the elbow joint.

71

SPINNING HOOK KICK

A spinning hook kick is used to hit the side of an opponent's head. When the attack is executed, the attacker's foot will be flexed with the toes pointing away from the head and it is the heel of the foot that connects with the opponent's head. As this is a spinning kick, the attacker must first make a 360 degree rotation: the attacker shifts their lead foot to the side (towards the direction of the spin) and starts spinning. Once the attacker is past 180 degrees, they start lifting their rear leg up in preparation for the attack with the side of the foot pointing towards the ceiling. The attacker continues to spin until they make contact with the opponent's head. The spinning hook kick is very similar to the spinning axe kick except the part of the foot that makes contact with the head. This kick can be done off both legs, however, some clubs focus only on the strongest leg or side.

72

STANCE

The Kickboxing stance is the same as the Boxing stance. One foot is in front of the other, both are pointing to the right (for a right-handed person) at a 45 degree angle. The stance is not too long, but is not as short as a Muay Thai stance. The two feet can be thought of as two diagonally opposite points of a rectangle. Although this is the standard Kickboxing stance, some practitioners opt for slightly varied versions depending on whether they are kicking or punching.

73

STRAIGHT RIGHT

Straight right is another term used for a cross. The cross is a straight, right-handed punch (if the practitioner is right-handed). It is usually stronger than the jab, but not necessarily as quick. To improve the power of the cross, the practitioner will pivot on their rear foot (and turn the upper body) so that the knee and toes are pointing in the direction of the punch as the fist makes contact with the target.

74

SWAY BACK

Sway back is a form of evasive move used when defending against punches to the head or possibly kicks to the head. For example, when the attacker jabs to the head, the defender keeps their feet still, but leans their upper body back in order to evade the attack. This defence is only effective if the defender is not too close to the attacker.

75

SWITCH CHANGE ROUNDHOUSE KICK

A switch change roundhouse kick is a roundhouse kick that is executed off the lead leg instead of the rear leg. In order for this kick to be executed, the practitioner's stance needs to change, so the lead leg becomes the rear leg. In order to switch the stance, the practitioner raises their lead foot off the ground slightly, steps it back to be adjacent to the rear foot, then steps the rear foot forward as to take the place of the lead foot. After the switch of leads, the practitioner then does a roundhouse kick. The roundhouse kick is an attack using the shin. The attacker pivots on their new lead foot about 90 degrees in order to get momentum behind the kick. The new rear leg is quite straight, but there is a slight bend in the leg. Roundhouse kicks are either aimed at the body (rib area) or the head.

76

TRIPLE JAB

See 'jab' for information on a single jab or 'double jab' for information on a double jab. A triple jab is three consecutive jabs. After the first jab, the attacker can either pull their hand all the way back to their guard position before the second and third jabs or pull their hand back about halfway. This is usually down to the preference of the practitioner.

77

UPPERCUTS

Uppercuts are punches commonly aimed under the chin of the opponent. The attacker bends down so that their elbow can touch the top of their leg, then the attacker raises themselves up punching with either the lead or rear fist pointing towards the ceiling. This is an example of a close range uppercut. There are also medium range uppercuts when the attacker is not close enough to their opponent to execute a close range uppercut effectively. See 'medium range uppercuts' for more information.

PART 3:

BITS & PIECES

78

AMERICAN KICKBOXING

American Kickboxing evolved in the 1970s as a result of people who practiced Karate not being challenged enough in that art alone. Although Karate had effective kicks, practitioners realised that the punches were not nearly as effective as Western Boxing punches. Kickboxing became an amalgamation of several arts to make it a more effective system, especially when competing.

79

ASSOCIATIONS

Associations are organisations that cover more than just Kickboxing, although there are Kickboxing specific associations. Their role is to insure martial arts clubs/students, provide competitions/championships and usually a grading system for martial artists to work towards. There are numerous associations throughout the world for different martial arts resulting in there not just being one championship or grading system.

80

BAG WORK

Bag work involves using punch bags to practice different attacking combinations or specific punches and kicks. They are particularly useful for improving a practitioner's power as most punch bags are very hard and heavy.

81

BELTS

Belts are awarded to martial arts practitioners who are a working through a grading system. Belts come in a variety of colours and styles. There are one colour belts; two tone belts with one stripe; two tone belts with two stripes etc. Not all Kickboxing clubs offer a grading system and the ones that do usually have a different order of colours which is often as a result of being with different martial arts associations. Black belt is commonly the highest colour with the students then moving up the Black belt Dan or Degree grades.

82

BOW

Most martial arts have a bow which is executed at the beginning and end of a training session or class. The common bow used in Kickboxing is for the student to have their feet together, hands by their sides and bend forward slightly.

83

BREATHING

When punching and kicking in Kickboxing, it is important to breathe properly to build the core correctly. As a practitioner punches, they must ensure they breathe out. Sometimes the practitioner will make a slight noise when they punch or kick so that they know they have done the correct breathing.

84

COMPETITIONS

Kickboxing is a sport as much as it is a martial art. There are different types of competitions and slightly different rules depending on the organisation that is running them. In a competition, the two competitors cannot attack below the waist. The three main types of competition are 'Light Continuous', 'Semi-Contact' and 'Full Contact'.

85

DANS

If a club has a 'belt system' that a student can work their way up, the top belt colour is commonly black. Once a student achieves their black belt, it is then common for a club to have a hierarchy of black belts. They achieve this by having what are known as Dans. When a student reaches their first black belt, this is usually referred to as a 1st Dan. The next one up is the 2nd Dan and so on. These Dans can be represented as stripes embroidered onto the end of a black belt.

86

DEGREES

A Degree is the same as a Dan. Different clubs use the alternative term if their martial art(s) has origins that would make Degree the more appropriate term than Dan. If a club has a 'belt system' that a student can work their way up, the top belt colour is commonly black. Once a student achieves their black belt, it is then common for a club to have a hierarchy of black belts. They achieve this by having what are known as Degrees. When a student reaches their first black belt, this is usually referred to as a 1st Degree. The next one up is the 2nd Degree and so on. These Degrees can be represented as stripes embroidered onto the end of a black belt.

87

DOJO

The term 'dojo' originates from Japan. In the West, dojo refers to the training place for practitioners to train in their chosen martial art. Other martial arts can sometimes use a different name for their training room depending on where they came from.

88

FULL CONTACT

Full Contact competitions are similar to Light Continuous except they are performed in a ring as opposed to a mat. There are a minimum of two rounds and a maximum of three rounds. Each round is two minutes long with a one minute break in between. There are usually three judges presiding over the fight. The fight is marked on a points system called the 'tens ruling system'. The competitors will score between eight and ten points in the fight. Ten points are awarded if the judges think the fighter performed exceptionally well, nine points for a great performance and eight points for an average demonstration. A point is sometimes deducted from a fighter if they foul. This can lead a fighter to only get seven points on occasion.

89

GRADES

Grades are a form of assessment that is sometimes used in clubs to determine the level of the student. This is commonly in the form of a belt system, but not always. Grades are a great way for a student to focus on an achievable goal, but sometimes focussing too much on grades alone can cause a student to not completely develop in that martial art.

90

GRANDMASTER

Some clubs use the terms Master and Grandmaster when Black belts get to a high enough Dan or Degree to show their level of experience in that art. A practitioner commonly reaches the level of Grandmaster when they are an 8th Dan or above.

91

JAPANESE KICKBOXING

Japanese Kickboxing was created in the 1960s and was the first style of Kickboxing to emerge. Japanese Kickboxing is much more similar to Muay Thai than American Kickboxing, for example. Japanese Kickboxing allows for knees, elbows, clinching, attacking below waist height (other Kickboxing styles do not allow for any attacks below the waist). However, in more recent years, the use of elbows and clinching has been disallowed from the Kickboxing style.

92

KICKBOXING

Kickboxing is a martial art which has been derived from several other martial arts over time. Different clubs and regions in the world have slightly different variants of the same art. The variant of Kickboxing described in this book has been derived from Karate, Muay Thai and Boxing and uses only punches and kicks, whereas some forms use elbows and knees as well.

93

LIGHT CONTINUOUS

Light Continuous competitions consist of one round that usually lasts two minutes. The fight is done on mats rather than in a ring and the contact is between light and heavy. There are three or four judges and no points involved. When the round is over, the judges close their eyes and raise their left or right arm depending on which fighter they think won. If a judge thinks it was a draw, they raise their arms in a cross shape in front of them. If there are more 'right' votes than 'left' votes then the competitor on the right would win. If there are all 'draw' votes or equal 'right' and 'left' votes then they would repeat the round to get a decisive result. The judges close their eyes before giving the result in order not to copy the decision of another judge and keep it as fair as possible.

94

MASTER

Some clubs use the terms Master and Grandmaster when Black belts get to a high enough Dan or Degree to show their level of experience in that art. A practitioner commonly reaches the level of Master when they are a 5th Dan or above.

95

ORIGIN

Kickboxing does not have a clear origin. Japanese Kickboxing has taken a lot of influences from Thailand and Muay Thai/Muay Boran. American Kickboxing combines more Western Boxing and Karate. There are other forms of Kickboxing which draw influences again from other martial arts.

96

RESPECT

Martial arts training can be beneficial in building up more respect over time. There are many ways that respect is demonstrated throughout a training session. In some clubs, it is common to bow when entering or exiting the dojo; students bow to their partner at the beginning and end of a round or training session; students bow at the beginning and end of a class; practitioners touch gloves with their opponent just before sparring. Some clubs require the instructor to be called Sir/Ma'am, Sensei or Master.

97

SEMI-CONTACT

Semi-Contact is a different form of competition from Light Continuous or Full Contact. Semi-Contact is completely based on points. Punches reaching their target usually score one point and kicks score more, but vary. The minimum amount of points a fighter has to get to in order to finish the fight is five and the maximum is first to ten. The fight lasts for two minutes. If there is a draw after two minutes, the fighters will go into extra time. If there is still no definite winner then they go into sudden death. There are usually two judges presiding over a Semi-Contact fight.

98

SENPEi

Senpei is the Japanese term for 'Assistant Instructor'. This can range from anyone who is not the top instructor of a club to someone who is close to becoming an instructor and are 'in training'.

99

SENSEi

Sensei is the Japanese term for 'Instructor'. Clubs with a belt grading system will call a black belt Sensei when they teach or the 'chief' instructor of a club. Some clubs require students to call the instructor Sensei even out of class.

UPCOMING BOOKS

- 99 Snippets of… Electric Guitar
- 99 Snippets of… Muay Thai
- 99 Snippets of… Amazing Foods
- 99 Snippets of… Bass Guitar
- 99 Snippets of… Jun Fan Gung Fu

More details can be found on our website:

www.dragonsnakepublishing.co.uk

ABOUT ALEXANDRA

Alexandra has two passions, martial arts and music both of which she has studied since childhood.

Alexandra is currently a 3rd Dan Black Belt in Kickboxing, a 2nd in Muay Thai and Jun Fan Gung Fu/JKD, a 1st in Kali/Filipino Martial Arts and also trains in MMA (Mixed Martial Arts), Judo, Sombo and Fencing. She is an Instructor and Senior Grading Examiner for UK MASDA (UK Martial Arts Self Defence Association) and has her own martial arts club (Dragon Snake Martial Arts) in Malmesbury, Wiltshire.

Musically she has dabbled with various instruments including the piano and saxophone but now concentrates on bass guitar, electric guitar and drums. During her time at University she was the bass player for Essex covers band, 31X.

* 9 7 8 0 9 5 7 1 7 0 6 0 5 *

ND - #0096 - 060826 - C0 - 148/105/6 - PB - 9780957170605 - Gloss Lamination